This book belongs to

Erin Stolhammer

May you enjoy many hours reading together!

God bless—

Pastor Dave & Judy
Britta & Scott

1986

BIG THOUGHTS
for little people

K E N N E T H · N · T A Y L O R

Illustrated by Kathryn E. Shoemaker

TYNDALE HOUSE PUBLISHERS, INC.
WHEATON, ILLINOIS

All Scripture verses in this book are from
The Living Bible, © 1971 by Tyndale House Publishers.

Seventh printing, September 1985

Library of Congress Catalog Card Number 83-50126
ISBN 0-8423-0164-X, cloth
Text, Copyright © 1983 by Kenneth N. Taylor
Artwork, Copyright © 1983 by Kathryn E. Shoemaker
Printed in the United States of America

A WORD TO PARENTS (and Grandparents)

Many years ago my little book *The Bible in Pictures for Little Eyes* was quietly introduced to Christian parents in America, and now there are a million copies in print in thirty languages around the world. My purpose was to help little children learn about the Bible and God.

This book, *Big Thoughts for Little People*, has a different purpose. Its value is in teaching small children about Christian living—that is, how to be good! This is one of the great themes of the Bible, and it is very important for little children to be taught right from wrong (as well as simple courtesy and good manners).

A word about the wonderful artwork is in order. There are surprises in every picture. For instance, how many ladybugs can you and your child find on the cover? (I see six of them!) There are ladybugs hiding in each illustration. You'll also have fun finding all the objects on each page which begin with the theme letter.

The questions are a very important part of each lesson. Questions that are thought-provoking but not hard to answer are of great importance in the learning process.

And please don't skip the Bible verses. Children will learn them easily, and they will stay in the mind and heart for life.

KENNETH N. TAYLOR

is for Asking.
We ask when we pray.
God's happy to answer
And help us each day.

The boy and his father are praying. Can you see them?
It is bedtime, and they are talking to God. They are asking
God to take care of them and they are saying, "Thank
you" for all the kind things God does for them. God wants us
to talk with him. He wants to be our friend. We can pray
anytime, wherever we are, because God always hears us.

SOME QUESTIONS TO ANSWER
1. What are the boy and his father doing?
2. Point to the bears who are thankful to God for their food.
3. What are some things you are thankful for? Let's pray
   now and tell God, "Thank you."

A BIBLE VERSE FOR YOU TO LEARN
Tell God your needs and don't forget to thank him for his answer.

PHILIPPIANS 4:6

B's for Behave;
It means doing what's right.
Be happy and helpful;
Don't argue or fight.

Do you know what "behave" means? It means doing what your parents ask you to do. It also means playing nicely with other children. In this picture some of the children and animals are behaving and some are not. Look at the girls fighting over an ice cream cone. I think the ice cream cone is going to fall to the ground. Then neither of the girls will have it. But the puppies know better. They are sharing.

SOME QUESTIONS TO ANSWER
1. Are the little girls behaving? What are they doing?
2. Point to the puppies. Are they behaving?
3. What are the children at the table doing?

A BIBLE VERSE FOR YOU TO LEARN
Jesus said, "If you love me, obey me." JOHN 14:15

C is for Crying.
It hurts when you fall,
But please do not cry
About nothing at all.

Can you see what happened to the little girls on the tricycles? They bumped into each other, and one girl has fallen off. Ouch! That hurts. Perhaps she bumped her head. I think she's going to cry. What would you do if you fell off? Would you cry? It's all right to cry if you're hurt. Crying will help you feel better. But if you're not really hurt, try to smile. Smiling will also help you feel better.

SOME QUESTIONS TO ANSWER
1. Why is the girl crying?
2. Is it all right to cry if you're hurt?
3. Should you cry every time you get a little bump?

A BIBLE VERSE FOR YOU TO LEARN
A cheerful heart does good like medicine. PROVERBS 17:22

D is for Doing
What needs to be done.
So please do it cheerfully;
Then you'll have fun.

All these children are doing nice things to help each other. One boy is helping the teacher wash the dishes. He must be careful not to drop and break them. One of the girls is helping by watering the flowers. One of the boys is pulling a girl and her bear in the wagon. We should treat others just as we want them to treat us. God is happy when we do helpful and kind things for one another.

SOME QUESTIONS TO ANSWER
1. What is the duck doing?
2. How are the children doing kind things for one another? Tell about each one.
3. What kind thing could you do to help someone?

A BIBLE VERSE FOR YOU TO LEARN
Do for others what you want them to do for you. MATTHEW 7:12

E is for Everyone.
God loves us all:
The black and the white,
And the short and the tall.

Everyone in the world is special to God. We are all different, but he loves all of us. There are many colors of hair and many colors of skin. Some children are tall, some are short. Some are fat, some are thin. In this country we live in houses or apartments. In some countries, the children live in houses made of straw or bamboo. Do you see all of the different children playing together in the picture? God loves all of them.

SOME QUESTIONS TO ANSWER
1. What color is your hair?
2. Find the boy driving the train. What color is his hair?
3. Does God love all the children? Does God love you?

A BIBLE VERSE FOR YOU TO LEARN
See how very much our heavenly Father loves us, for he allows us

to be called his children. 1 JOHN 3:1

's for Forgive
If a girl or a boy
Is naughty or careless
And breaks your new toy.

Do you see what the bear has done? He has broken the toy frog. If someone did that to you, you might be angry. Perhaps you would want to get even with him by doing something bad to him. But that isn't the way God wants you to act. He wants you to forgive. He does not want you to hurt people who do something wrong to you. He wants you to be good to them. That isn't easy, but God will help you.

SOME QUESTIONS TO ANSWER
1. Look at the children playing in the sandbox. What are they doing?
2. Should those children continue fighting, or should they forgive each other?
3. Did someone hurt you or hurt your feelings today? Did you forgive him?

A BIBLE VERSE FOR YOU TO LEARN
Be kind to each other, tenderhearted, forgiving one another. EPHESIAN.

is for God;
He's your Father above.
He made you and likes you
And shows you his love.

God lives in heaven, far up above the sky, but he is also here with us. Can you see God in the picture? No, we can't see him, but he can see us. He loves us and always wants to help us. He made the earth and sky and flowers and everything there is. But even though he is so great and strong, he thinks about us all the time. He wants us to think about him and love him too.

SOME QUESTIONS TO ANSWER
1. Who made the flowers? Who made you?
2. Where is God? Can you see him? Can he see you?
3. Does God love you? Do you love him?

A BIBLE VERSE FOR YOU TO LEARN
The Lord God made the earth and the heavens. GENESIS 2:4

H is for Helping
Your mother or dad.
It says in the Bible
That this makes God glad.

God tells us in the Bible to be kind to others and to help them. Sometimes that isn't easy, because we want to do things to please ourselves instead of helping others. Look at all the children in the picture who are helping. Some are helping collect eggs. Others are helping with the small animals. God wants us to be cheerful helpers. That means not to complain when you are asked to help. God will help you be a cheerful helper if you ask him to.

SOME QUESTIONS TO ANSWER
1. Point to all the children who are helping. What is each one doing?
2. Were you a helper today? What did you do?
3. What can you do tomorrow to be a helper? Ask your mother or father to remind you to be a helper.

A BIBLE VERSE FOR YOU TO LEARN
God will bless you and use you to help others. 1 TIMOTHY 4:16

is for Illness,
It keeps you in bed.
But soon you'll feel fine
And be playing instead.

It isn't fun to be sick, but it happens to all of us once in awhile. Usually you feel better soon, but sometimes you need to go to the doctor to get medicine or a shot. You might even have to go to the hospital. Some children live in countries where there aren't very many doctors to help. In those countries the children are sick more often and sometimes it takes much longer for them to get well. Isn't it wonderful to live where there are doctors to help us? We should thank God for doctors when we pray.

SOME QUESTIONS TO ANSWER
1. Have you ever been sick?
2. Did you go to the doctor?
3. What did the doctor do?

A BIBLE VERSE FOR YOU TO LEARN
I was sick and you visited me. MATTHEW 25:36

J is for Joyful;
It means full of cheer.
Have fun and be happy
Each day of the year.

Christmas is a joyful time. It is the celebration of Jesus' birthday. It reminds us about God and how much he loves us. We decorate Christmas trees and give presents to each other. We like to sing Christmas carols. We can also be joyful every day of the year. We can thank God for our families. We can play with our friends. We can help other people. These things all make us joyful.

SOME QUESTIONS TO ANSWER
1. What kind of tree is in the picture?
2. Are the children in the picture being joyful or sad?
3. What are some things that make you joyful?

A BIBLE VERSE FOR YOU TO LEARN
Always be full of joy in the Lord. PHILIPPIANS 4:4

K is for Kindness
To Grandpa and Gram;
Be helpful to others,
Be sweet as a lamb!

These children are visiting their grandparents and are being kind to them. Being kind means being friendly to people and helping them. Some people are mean and not kind at all. They want everything for themselves. They don't stop to think about what other people want. When they act that way, they are being unkind. But God wants us to help others and to be friendly to them. He wants us to be kind.

SOME QUESTIONS TO ANSWER
1. Have you ever been mean and unkind? Tell about it.
2. Tell about something you did to be kind to someone.
3. Does God want you to be kind or unkind?

A BIBLE VERSE FOR YOU TO LEARN
You should practice tenderhearted mercy and kindness to others.

COLOSSIANS 3:12

L is for Lying,
A thing not to do.
No matter what happens,
Don't say what's not true.

Look at the broken window. The boy's baseball went through the window. Have you ever broken something and then said you didn't do it? That would be lying instead of telling the truth, and God doesn't like lies. I hope the boy tells the truth about the broken window. Why do people tell lies? I think it is because they don't want to be scolded or punished for what they have done. But God wants us to tell the truth, even if it means we will be punished.

SOME QUESTIONS TO ANSWER
1. What happened to the window?
2. Does God want us to tell lies?
3. Can you think of a time when you wanted to tell a lie, but told the truth instead?

A BIBLE VERSE FOR YOU TO LEARN
You must not lie. EXODUS 20:16

M is for Messy,
With toys on the floor;
So pick them up neatly
When playtime is o'er.

Some boys and girls leave their toys on the floor where people can fall over them and get hurt and break the toys. Wouldn't it be better to pick up the toys and put them away when you are through playing with them? Usually this makes everyone happier. It is also good to make your bed look neat in the morning and after a nap. And you can clear the table after meals and help wash and dry the dishes so they won't be messy.

SOME QUESTIONS TO ANSWER
1. What is the girl doing to her bed?
2. What should the children do with the toys on the floor?
3. Do you pick up your toys when you are finished playing with them?

A BIBLE VERSE FOR YOU TO LEARN
God is not one who likes things to be disorderly and upset. 1 CORI

THIANS 14:33

N is for Nice;
It is always worthwhile.
Be pleasant to others
And give them a smile.

Do your parents ever tell you to be nice? What do they mean? Perhaps you have been playing too roughly or have hit someone or been quarreling. When they tell you to be nice they mean you should stop doing those things. They want you to be pleasant and helpful. When you are nice, everyone is happy. When you do something naughty, everyone is sad.

SOME QUESTIONS TO ANSWER
1. Did you do anything today that wasn't nice? What was it?
2. Did you do something nice today? What was it?
3. What can you do tomorrow to be nice?

A BIBLE VERSE FOR YOU TO LEARN
Happy are the kind and merciful. MATTHEW 5:7

O's for Obey.
When you do as you're told,
It makes parents glad;
They won't spank you or scold.

God tells us to obey our parents. He says this is very important because our parents know what is best for us. We will be happiest if we obey our parents. God says that fathers and mothers should punish their children when they don't obey. If you are punished, it will help you remember to obey your parents. And after they have punished you, your parents will give you a big hug and will tell you how much they love you. Then everyone will be happy.

SOME QUESTIONS TO ANSWER
1. Where do you think the little girl is going?
2. What does God say your parents should do if you don't obey?
3. Who is happy when you obey?

A BIBLE VERSE FOR YOU TO LEARN
Children, obey your parents. This is the right thing to do. EPHESIAN

P's for Polite,
Saying, "Thank you" and "Please."
It's easy to do
And puts others at ease.

When you ask for something, it is more polite to say, "May I please have it?" than to say, "Gimme that!" And when someone gives you something, it is polite to say, "Thank you." Being polite shows respect. That means you think the other person is as good as you are, or even better. God wants us to respect other people, so he likes it when we are polite. He doesn't want us to think we are better than others.

SOME QUESTIONS TO ANSWER
1. Point to the children in the picture who are being polite.
2. Tell some ways you can be polite.
3. Does God want us to be polite? Why?

A BIBLE VERSE FOR YOU TO LEARN
Honor your father and mother. EPHESIANS 6:2

Q is for Quarrel;
Each wants the first turn.
But waiting for others
Is not hard to learn.

Oh, dear me! Look at those children quarreling. Each one is mad at everyone else! Is this good? No! Everyone is being selfish and wants things for himself instead of sharing with the others. Is there a way to solve their problem? I hope someone shows them how to play nicely together. You can learn to share and be kind to your playmates. Then they will learn to share too. You can be the one to show them how to share.

SOME QUESTIONS TO ANSWER
1. Why are the children in the picture quarreling?
2. Do you ever quarrel? About what?
3. How can you stop a quarrel?

A BIBLE VERSE FOR YOU TO LEARN
Quarreling, harsh words, and dislike of others should have no place

n your lives. EPHESIANS 4:31

R is for Resting,
Like taking a nap,
Or sometimes just sitting
On mother's soft lap.

Sometimes we all need to stop working or playing to take a rest. That is the way God made us. He wants us to be rested because then we are happier. If you don't get enough rest you will probably be cross and unhappy. Then everyone else will be unhappy too. Nap time is a good time. You can lie in bed and think pleasant thoughts, and all of a sudden you'll be asleep. Then when you wake up you'll be happy as a songbird. Maybe you will sing!

SOME QUESTIONS TO ANSWER
1. How many children in the picture are resting?
2. Why do you feel better after your nap?
3. What can happen when you get too tired?

A BIBLE VERSE FOR YOU TO LEARN
God wants his loved ones to get their proper rest. PSALM 127:2

S is for Singing;
We sing when we're glad.
It might even help you
To sing when you're sad.

Everyone likes to sing. There are happy songs and sad songs, funny songs and serious songs. We can sing while we play or while we take a walk. Some people like to sing in the bathtub or in the shower. God likes to hear us sing. He made us with voices that can sing. Singing makes us happy, and God wants us to be happy. Singing can even help us feel happy when we are sad. I hope you know lots of songs.

SOME QUESTIONS TO ANSWER
1. Which child is dressed up like a ladybug?
2. Do you like to sing?
3. What are some songs you know?

A BIBLE VERSE FOR YOU TO LEARN
Sing to the Lord with thankful hearts. COLOSSIANS 3:16

T is for Thankful;
Thank God for your lunch,
And thank him for dinner
And breakfast and brunch.

The children in the picture are thanking God for their food. Many children in the world don't have enough to eat. They are hungry all the time. But we have good breakfasts and lunches and suppers, and sometimes even snacks in between. So we should thank God every day that we have enough to eat. That's why we bow our heads before we eat and say, "Thank you" to God.

SOME QUESTIONS TO ANSWER
1. What are some things you are thankful for?
2. Who are some people you are thankful for?
3. When should we thank God for food?

A BIBLE VERSE FOR YOU TO LEARN
Thank the Lord for all the glorious things he does. PSALM 105:1

U's for Unselfish;
Be willing to share.
Be thoughtful of others
And always be fair.

A selfish person wants the first turn, the biggest cookie, and the best of everything. But an unselfish person is willing to let others go first or have the biggest cookie. When you share with your friends, you have more fun together. Sometimes it is very difficult, but God wants us to be unselfish, so that is the best thing to do. It is better to please God than to please ourselves. One good thing about sharing is that an unselfish person is happier than a selfish person.

SOME QUESTIONS TO ANSWER
1. Who is riding a unicycle?
2. Does God want us to be selfish or unselfish?
3. Can you think of some ways you can be unselfish?

A BIBLE VERSE FOR YOU TO LEARN
Don't think only of yourself. Try to think of the other person, too,

and what is best for him. 1 CORINTHIANS 10:24

V is for Visitors;
Help them have fun,
And play and be friendly
With all, not just one.

It is wonderful to have friends. You can go to their house to
visit, or they can come to visit you. Sometimes you can eat
lunch together, or you can play outside or have fun making
things. When you have visitors you must remember to
play happily together and take turns with your toys. And
remember to play with each of your visitors, not just the ones
you like best. Then everyone will have fun.

SOME QUESTIONS TO ANSWER
1. How many children in the picture are coming to visit?
2. Tell the names of your friends who come to your house to
   visit.
3. What are some things you do together?

A BIBLE VERSE FOR YOU TO LEARN
Cheerfully share your home with those who need a meal or a place

to stay for the night. *1 PETER 4:9*

W's for Worship—
That's giving God praise
And telling our love for him
All of our days.

When you think about how great and good God is, and how much you love him, then you are worshiping him. You can thank God and worship him at church, or at home, or when you are all alone. Yes, you can talk to God wherever you are. You can think about how wonderful he is because he made the trees and grass and stars and sun and moon. And you can tell him, "Thank you" for making you and loving you.

SOME QUESTIONS TO ANSWER
1. In the picture, which things did God make?
2. Who loves you even more than your parents do?
3. Tonight when you go to bed you can worship God by thanking him for loving you and for making the sun and stars.

A BIBLE VERSE FOR YOU TO LEARN
All the earth shall worship you and sing of your glories. PSALM 66:4

X is for Xylophone—
Use it to play
Happy songs about Jesus
Throughout each new day.

Look at all the musical instruments in this picture. Can you find the xylophones? Have you ever played a xylophone? It makes pretty music, but it sounds very different from a piano or a violin. Do you think God likes to hear children play a xylophone? I think he does. God likes music. He especially likes it when we play or sing songs about him. He wants us to tell him how much we love him.

SOME QUESTIONS TO ANSWER
1. Have you ever played a xylophone?
2. What other instruments are the children playing?
3. Does God like to hear children making music?

A BIBLE VERSE FOR YOU TO LEARN
Make a joyful symphony before the Lord, the King. PSALM 98:6

Y is for Yelling—
It's all right outdoors;
But please be more quiet
In houses and stores.

Do you like to yell? I think most children do. Sometimes making a lot of noise is all right, but sometimes it isn't. Here are some times you should be quiet:

When your mother is resting or is tired.
When the baby is asleep.
When your parents have guests.
When you should be taking a nap.

SOME QUESTIONS TO ANSWER
1. Who is taking a nap in the hammock?
2. Who is sleeping in the tree?
3. When should you be quiet?

A BIBLE VERSE FOR YOU TO LEARN
If you shout a pleasant greeting to a friend too early in the morning

e will count it as a curse! PROVERBS 27:14

Z is for Zebra
Or Zebu or Zoo.
God made all the creatures,
And he made you, too.

Do you know what a zoo is? It is a place where there are many, many kinds of animals and birds and snakes. There are even lions and tigers and bears. Have you ever been to a zoo? If so, you know how many kinds of animals there are. See if you can find some of them in the picture. Did you know that God made all these animals? God made the grass and trees and rocks and animals, and he made you a very special person.

SOME QUESTIONS TO ANSWER
1. Where are the zebras in the picture?
2. Which animals can the children pet?
3. Who made all the animals?

A BIBLE VERSE FOR YOU TO LEARN
The Lord said, "By my great power I have made the earth and all

mankind and every animal." JEREMIAH 27:5

ABOUT THE AUTHOR

Kenneth N. Taylor is best known as the translator of *The Living Bible,* but his first renown was as a writer of children's books. Ken and his wife Margaret have ten children, and his early books were written for use in the family's daily devotions. The manuscripts were ready for publication only when they passed the scrutiny of those ten young critics! Those books, which have now been read to two generations of children around the world, include *The Bible in Pictures for Little Eyes* (Moody Press), *Stories for the Children's Hour* (Moody Press), and *Taylor's Bible Story Book* (Tyndale House). Now the Taylor children are all grown, so *Big Thoughts for Little People* was written with the numerous grandchildren in mind.

Ken Taylor is a graduate of Wheaton College and Northern Baptist Seminary. He is the founder and president of Tyndale House Publishers, Inc. He and Margaret live in Wheaton, Illinois.

ABOUT THE ILLUSTRATOR

Kathryn E. Shoemaker has had broad experience as an art teacher, curriculum specialist, filmmaker, and illustrator. Her published works include twelve books, eight filmstrips, illustrations for many magazine articles, and numerous educational in-service materials. She is a strong advocate of the involvement of parents in the local schools, and spends a great deal of time as a volunteer in her children's school.

Kathryn is a graduate of Immaculate Heart College in Los Angeles. She also studied at Chouinards Art Institute, Otis Art Institute, and Occidental College, and is a member of the Society of Illustrators. She and her two children, Kristin and Andrew, who helped critique the illustrations for *Big Thoughts for Little People*, live in Vancouver, British Columbia.

C O L O P H O N

This book was designed by Tim Botts. The text type is Zapf International and was composed on a Mergenthaler VIP by Nora M. Holmes, Westmont, Illinois. The offset lithography for the cover, text, and endsheets was done by Dickinson Brothers, Inc., Grand Rapids, Michigan. The binding was done by Lake Book/John F. Cuneo, Inc., Melrose Park, Illinois. The text paper is a seventy pound white matte. The endsheet paper is eighty pound white smooth offset. The cover material is Permalin Boniflex embossed. Color separations for the cover were made by G & S Lithographers, Inc., Chicago, Illinois. Color separations for the endsheets and text were made by Magna Graphic, Inc., Lexington, Kentucky.